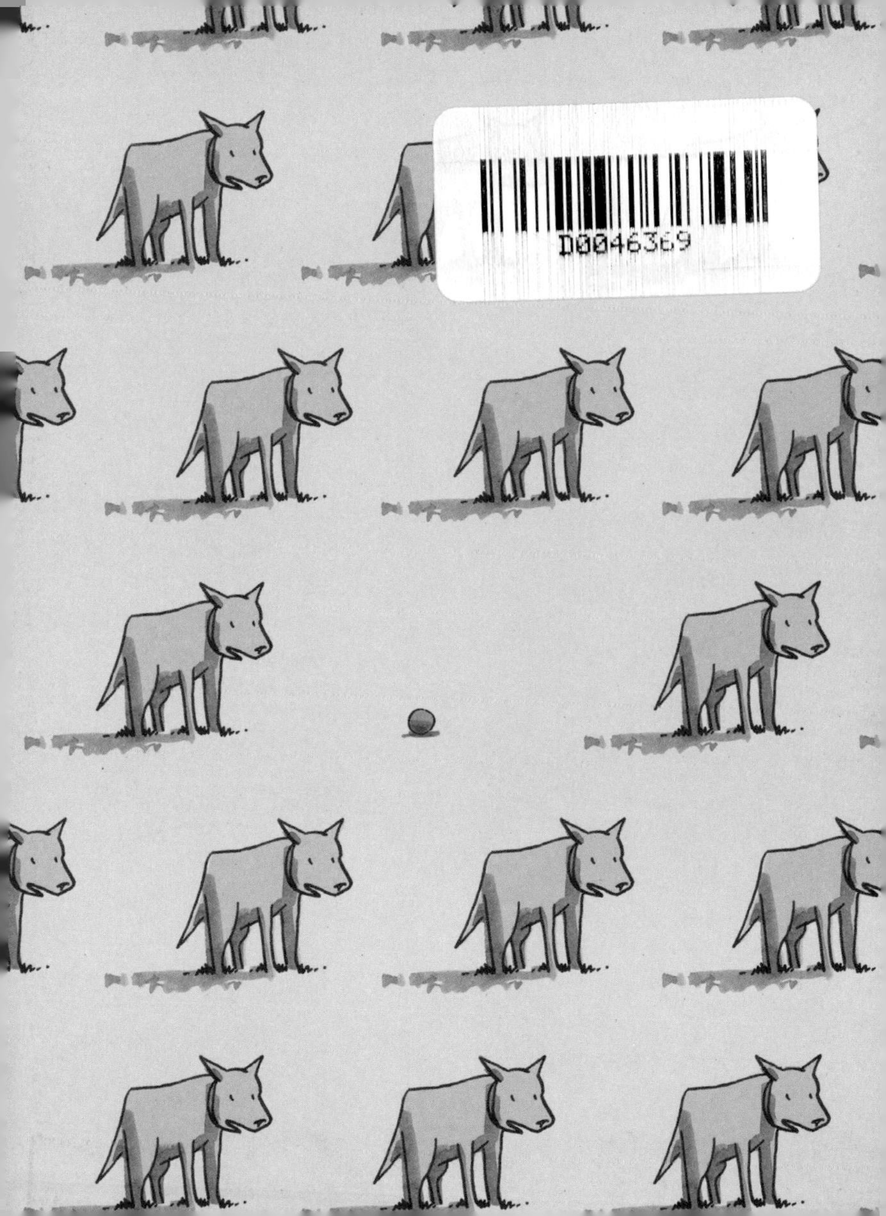

I Don't Get It™

I DON'T GET IT
Published by BOOM! Town,
An imprint of BOOM! Studios.

Copyright © 2010-2014 Shannon Wheeler.

Office of Publication
5670 Wilshire Boulevard, Suite 450
Los Angeles, CA 90036-5679

A catalog record for this book is available from OCLC and from the
BOOM! Studios website, www.boom-studios.com, on the Librarians page.

More information about Shannon Wheeler and his work can be found on
his website: www.tmcm.com
You can contact Shannon Wheeler at: cartoons@tmcm.com

FIRST HARDCOVER EDITION
January 2014
ISBN: 978-1-60886-405-8
EISBN: 978-1-61398-259-4

ASSISTANT EDITOR Jasmine Amiri
EDITOR Joan Hilty
BOOK DESIGN Hannah Nance Partlow

I Don't Get It.

SHANNON WHEELER
Introduction *by* Keith Knight

BOOM! Town is an imprint of BOOM! Studios

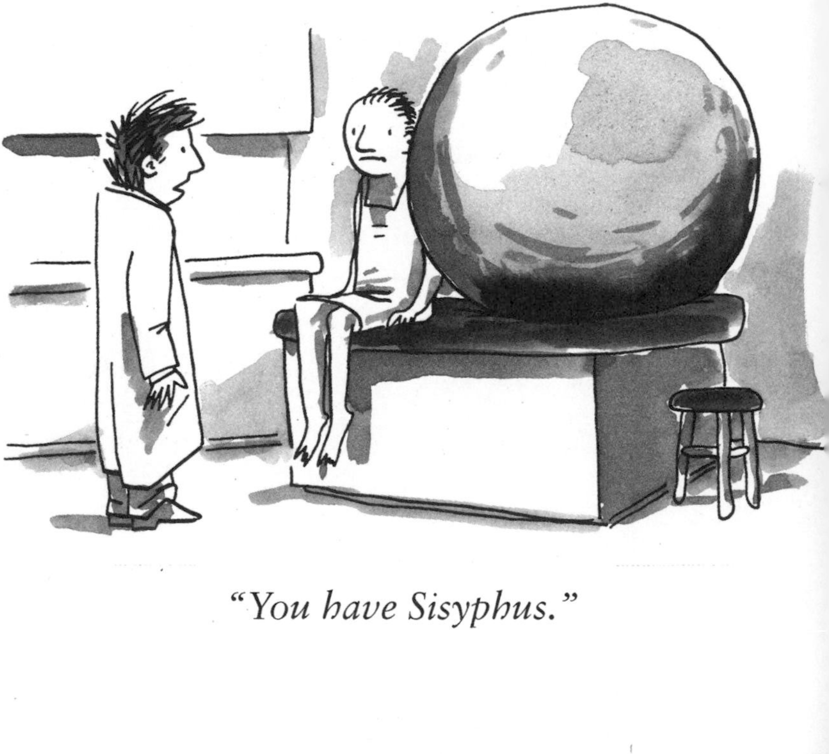

"You have Sisyphus."

✛ INTRODUCTION ✛

When my pregnant wife and I decided to check out Portland as a possible safe-drop spot following our adventures in L.A., the only place we thought about staying was Shannon Wheeler's house.

Why? In a word: COFFEE. Drinking coffee with Shannon Wheeler is like smoking a joint with Tommy Chong (I have done both). What do you expect from the man who gave the world *Too Much Coffee Man?*

Also, he and I are two peas in a pod. We're the peerest of peers. Shannon and I go way back. In fact, it was he who saddled me with the moniker of "Gentleman Cartoonist." I have tried to subvert and live up to that title ever since.

Shannon Wheeler is the Han Solo to my Lando Calrissian. Both of us are scoundrels. Hustlers. Cartoonists who began our careers during the zine wars of the early nineties. We may have never lived in the same town, but I have always kept an eye on Shannon. Shannon's success is my success.

And successful he has been. This is a man who once had Huey Newton as his landlord! Saw the Reverend Jim Jones TWICE, and lived to tell about it! Staged an opera based on his comic strip! He bought a house and raised two sweet kids on an indie cartoonist's salary! In a city that has more toonsters (and strip joints) per capita than any other city, he landed a gig on *Portlandia* as – get this – the cartoonist!

But his most amazing feat so far has been the transition from low-brow alt-weekly cartoonist to high-brow *New Yorker* cartoonist. And the thing is, his shit looks like it belongs there. Believe me, that ain't easy.

Here's what's so great about Shannon's single panels: they poke fun at such a wide swath of subject matter, while being drawn from so many different perspectives, that with every new one I gain a much deeper appreciation for him as a cartoonist and writer. So much deeper that I almost forget about the hustler/scoundrel part altogether.

So, God-speed, Shannon Wheeler. Keep on birthin' comics and babies (not necessarily in that order), and I'll look forward to sharing another bottle o' whiskey during our 50th anniversary panel at Comic-Con.

– Keith Knight
Los Angeles, CA

DENIAL

MEOOOOOOOOOOOOOOOOOO W.

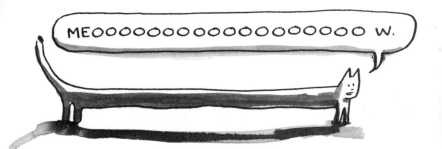

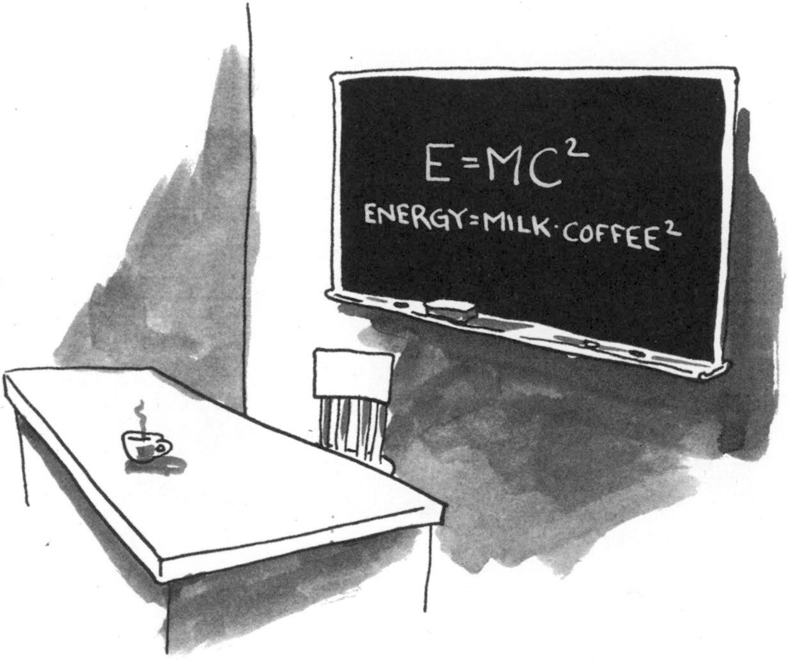
E = MC²
ENERGY = MILK · COFFEE²

8

Denial

"Before I introduce myself I'd like you to meet Debt, Anxiety, Anger,
Memory Loss, Male Pattern Baldness, Halitosis, Apathetic Relatives,
Distracted Doctor and Neglectful Nurse, Degrading Job,
Adulterous Wife, Mediocre Achievements, Profound Regret ..."

Denial

"You had me at your band name."

Denial

"I'd say it's worth about 900 words."

Denial

"We can't both write tell-all books."

Denial

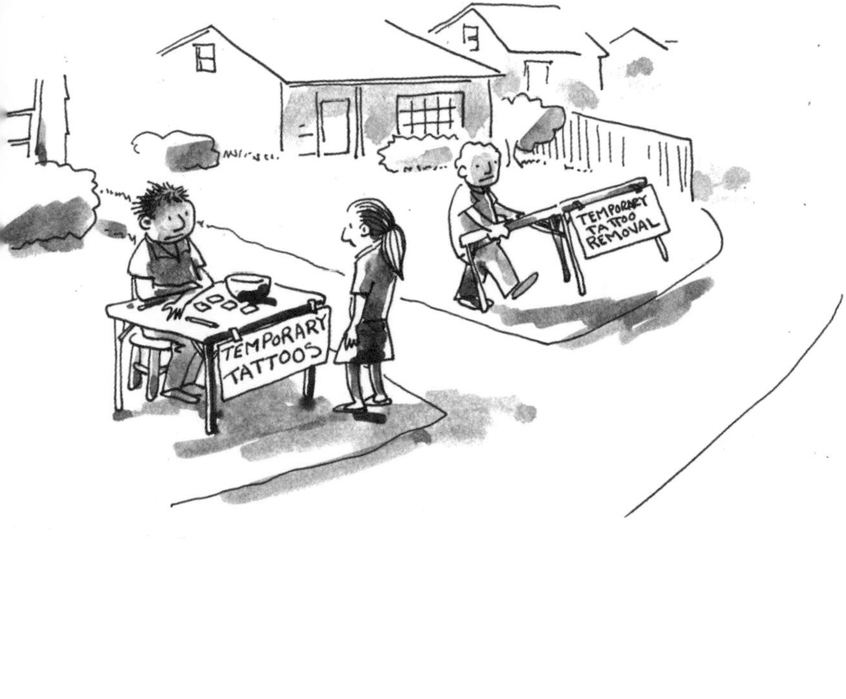
TEMPORARY
TATTOOS
TEMPORARY
TATTOO
REMOVAL

13

Denial

"Just ignore the morality clause."

Denial

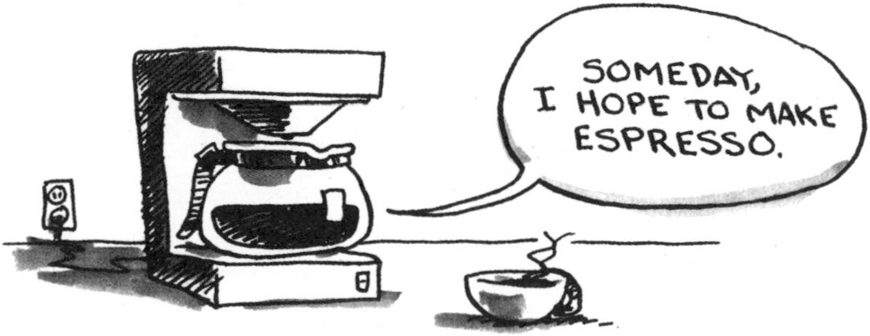
SOMEDAY, I HOPE TO MAKE ESPRESSO.

"But is it art?"

Denial

"Oh ye of little faith."

Denial

"He wants to be president when he grows up."

Denial

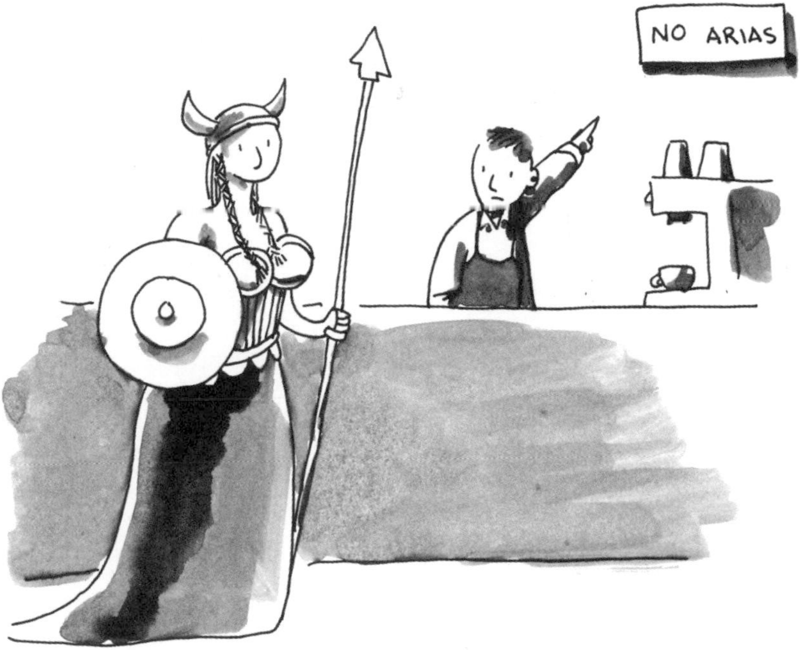
NO ARIAS

19

Denial

"Don't forget to write."

Denial

*"Even if we could vote,
the dog lobby isn't much to speak of."*

Denial

"Hey, free wifi."

Denial

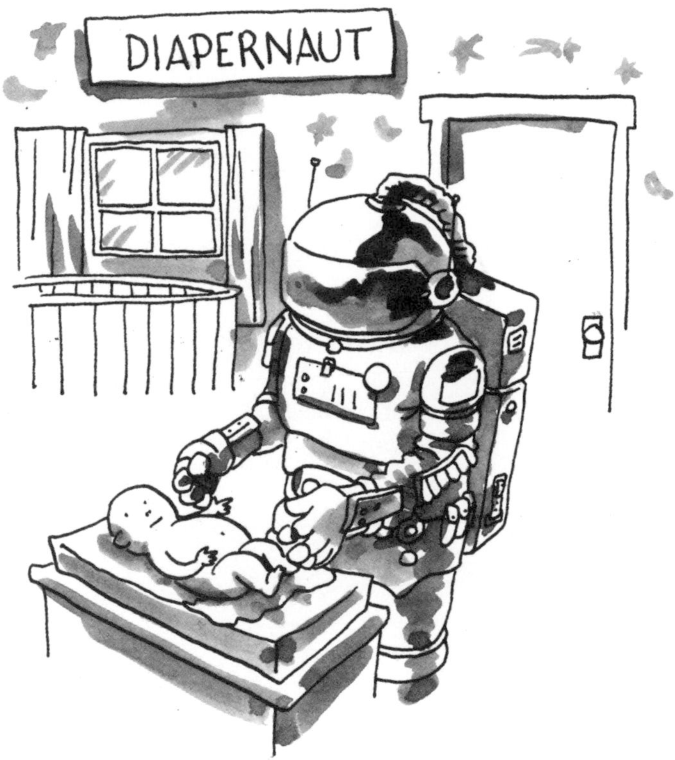
DIAPERNAUT

23

Denial

"I don't need legal representation for my bath."

Denial

Denial

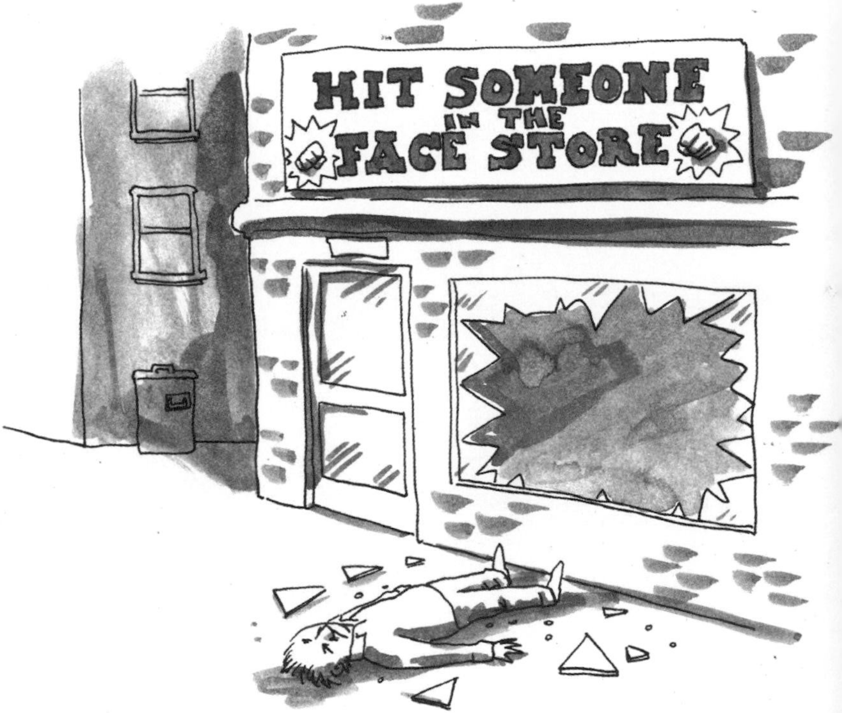
HIT SOMEONE
IN THE
FACE STORE

26

Denial

ANGER

KITTY LITTERER

"I don't care what the Mayan calendar said."

Anger

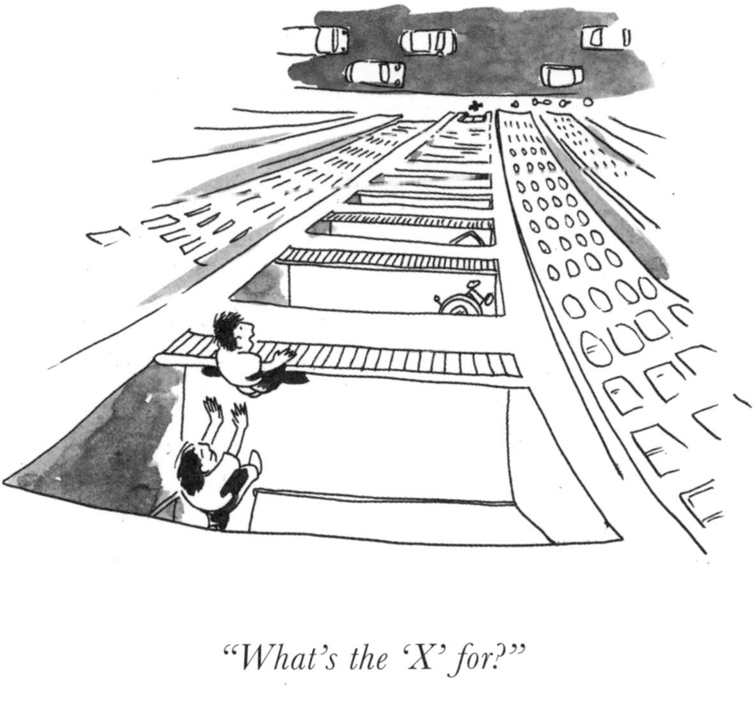

"What's the 'X' for?"

*"I didn't say you were fired.
I said I was letting you go."*

Anger

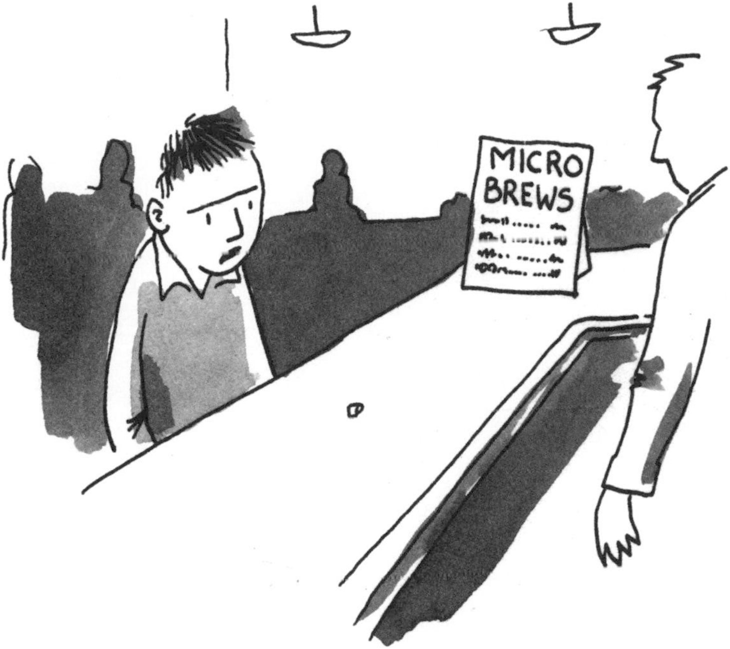
MICRO
BREWS

"Seriously?"

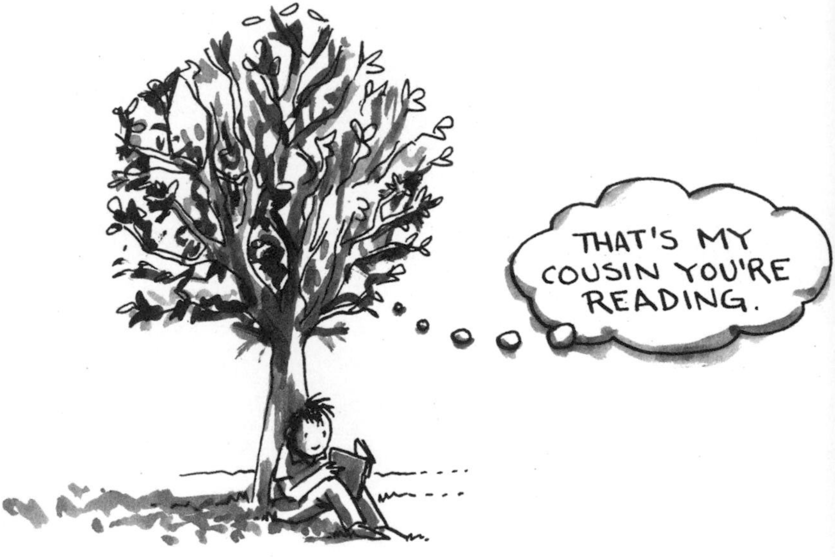
THAT'S MY COUSIN YOU'RE READING.

"Just so you know,
I'm following your 'live-tweeting' of our date."

Anger

"*I'm not autistic. I just don't like you.*"

Anger

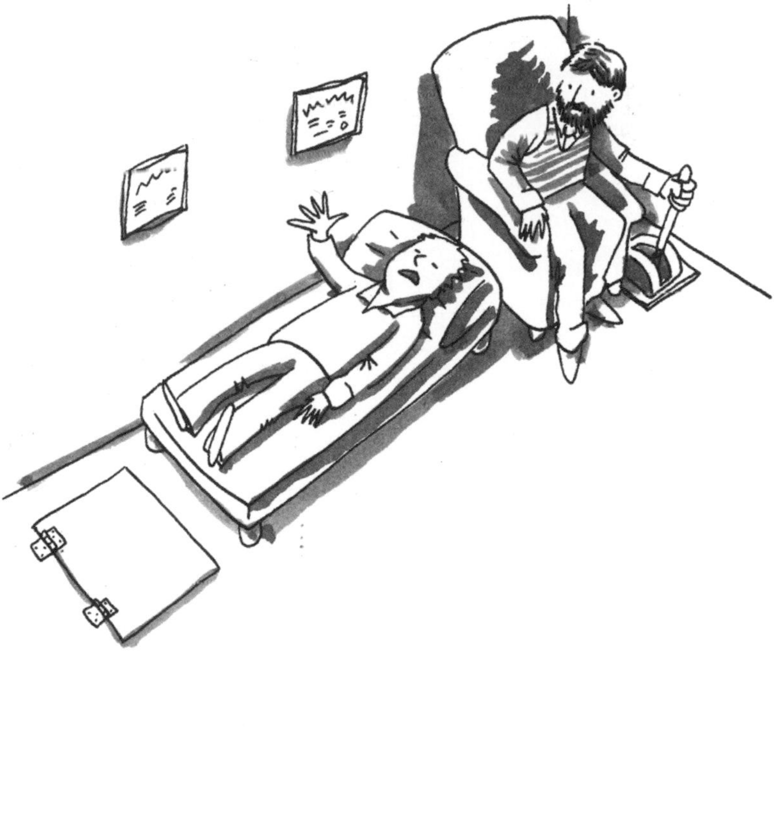

35

Anger

"Would you shut up?"

Anger

"You knew I was a blood donor
when you married me."

Anger

"I want you to apologize for that apology that wasn't an apology."

"We couldn't save your husband,
but we did save you some pizza."

Anger

"You're late."

Anger

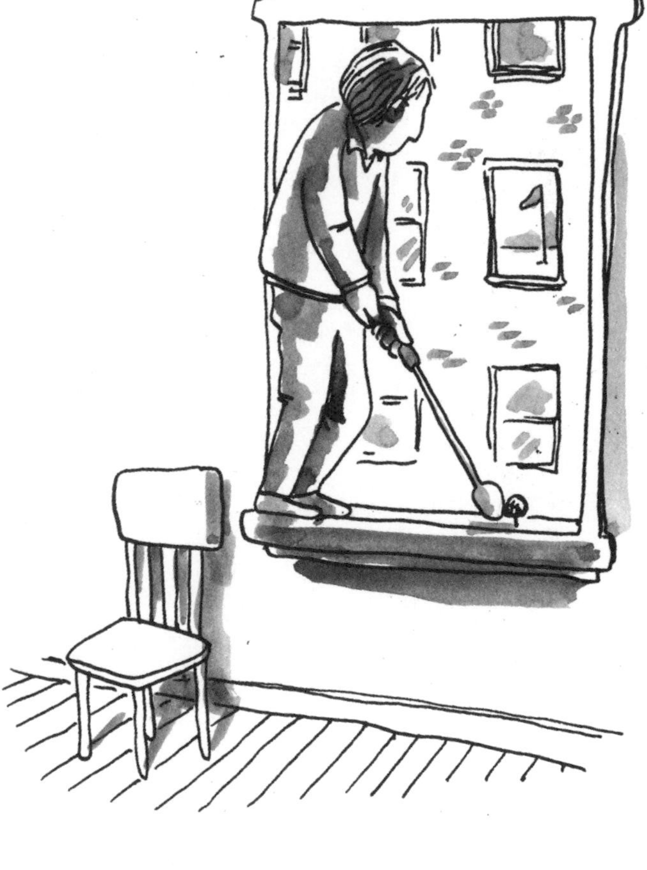

41

Anger

"No crowdsourcing."

"You better listen to me. I'm omnipotent."

43

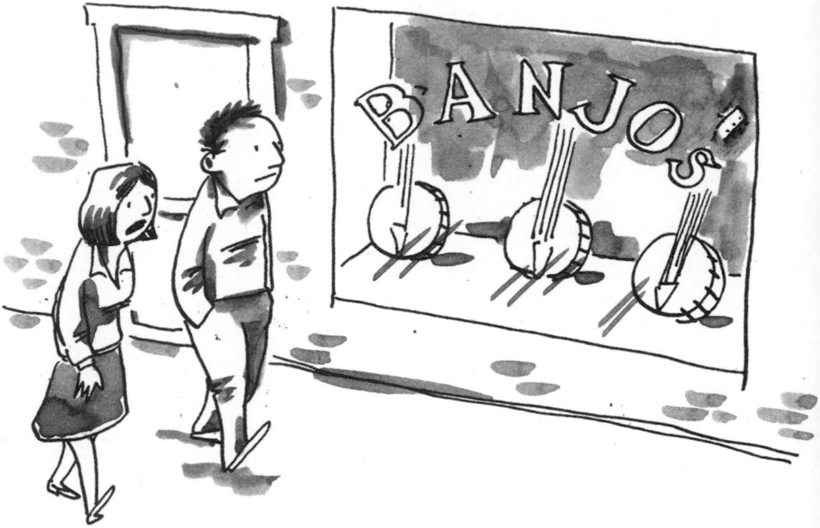
BANJOS

"No."

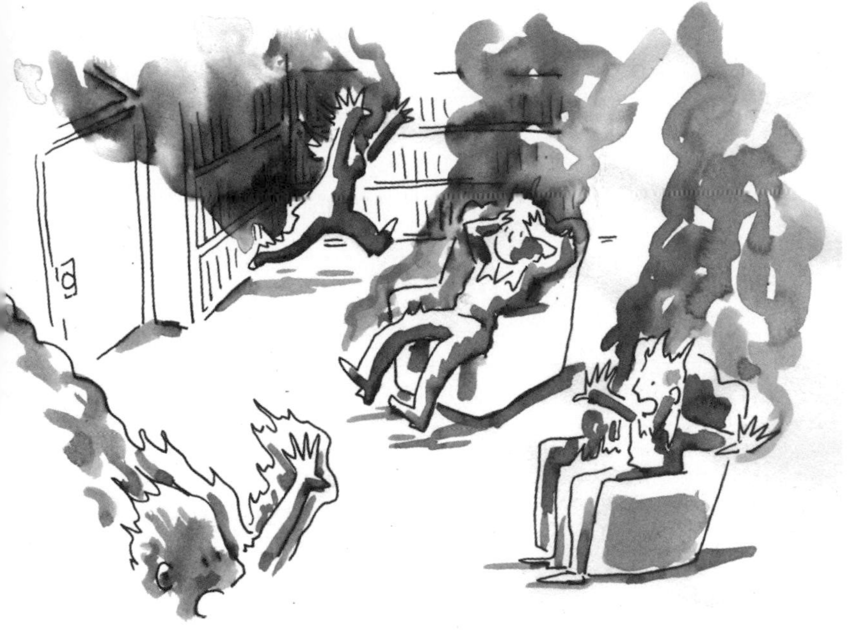

People-on-fire club.

"*What are these mice-chasing apps on my phone?*"

Anger

"*This is Ben and this is Ben's worst critic.*"

Anger

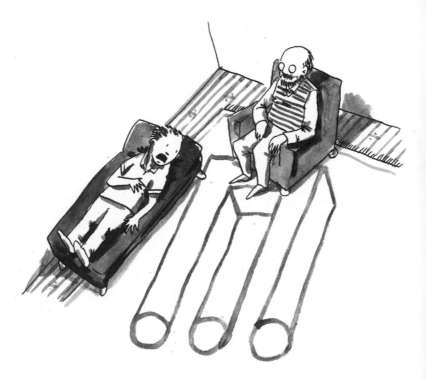

"Your rug. It's driving me crazy."

Anger

"*Have you tried turning it off and on again?*"

Anger

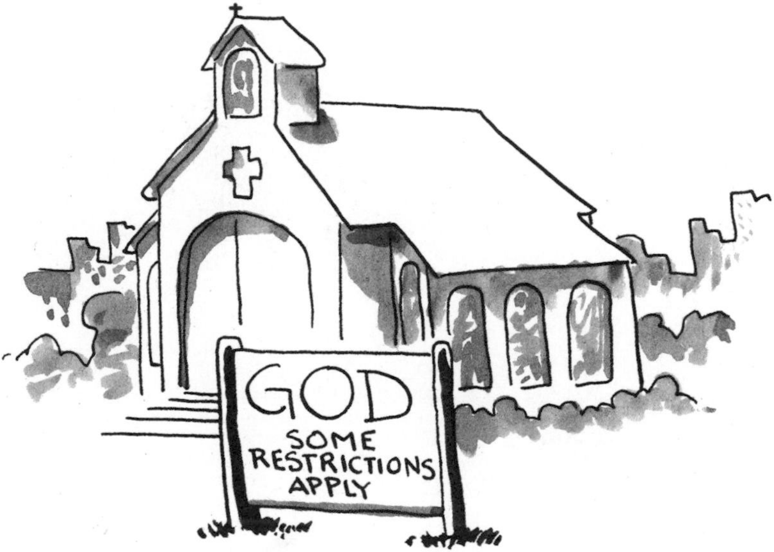
GOD
SOME
RESTRICTIONS
APPLY

BARGAINING

"How are you with cat toys?"

"Based on your viewing history, you might enjoy my other breast."

Bargaining

IF YOU HOLD AN AVOCADO TO YOUR EAR YOU CAN HEAR GUACAMOLE

"It's perfect. Let's take it."

"Thanks. We'll keep your résumé on file."

Bargaining

"What do the polls say?"

Bargaining

"I want to tell you about my Kickstarter."

"My homework was eaten with a light
red wine reduction sauce on a bed of
wild rice and shiitake mushroom pilaf with a
side of arugula and raspberry vinaigrette."

Bargaining

"Quick. Call an arborist."

"They were only here for 15 minutes."

Bargaining

"We the jury would like an option on the movie."

Bargaining

"You're lecturing."

Bargaining

"We're not getting a hellhound and that's final."

"*Forget building a fan site.
I want a sycophant site.*"

Bargaining

"Can I buy you a drink?"

Bargaining

"I think we should start seeing other people."

Bargaining

"I hope you'll consider
'liking' me on Facebook."

Bargaining

"What do you get someone who has everything?"

Bargaining

"*Random should be spelled differently every time.*"

Bargaining

"Tight on the reins."

OUT-OF-WORK MENTAL HEALTH
WORKERS AND LOBBYISTS
DISCUSS THE ROOT CAUSE OF
GUN VIOLENCE.

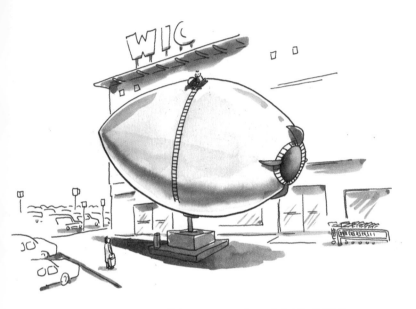

"*Mom, can I have another $813.66?*"

Bargaining

*"I thought life with you would
be more glamorous."*

74

DEPRESSION

"There was something on your x-ray,
but luckily it's still small."

Depression

"You realize our reputation is shot."

Depression

"For once I'd like change that isn't spare."

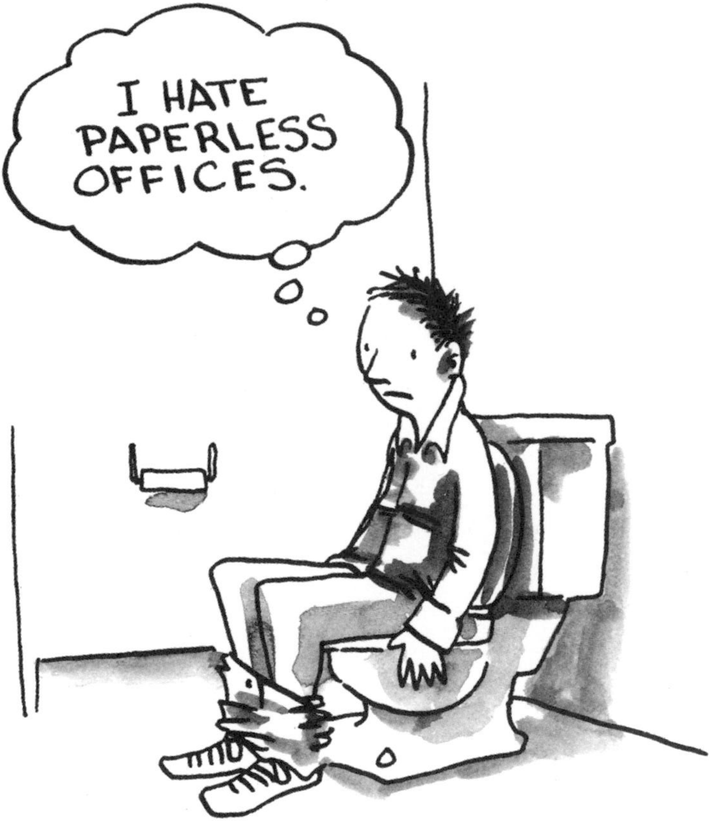
I HATE PAPERLESS OFFICES.

"This is not the place to get over fear of appearing in a cartoon."

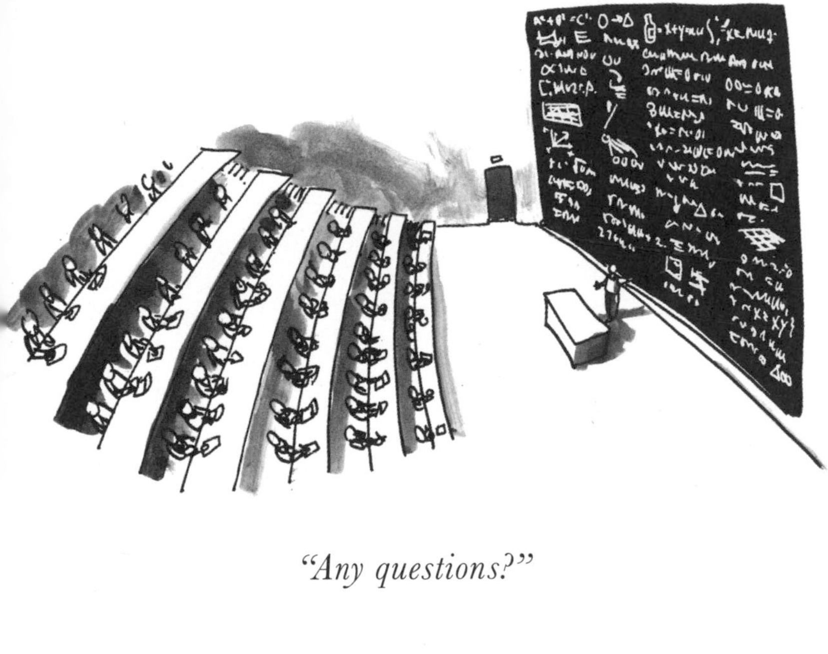

"Any questions?"

*"Careful, they possess technology
that makes you fat and lazy."*

Depression

"I used to be a millionaire but I lost it all when I invested heavily in a small piece of string."

Depression

"My attention span is too long for this."

Depression

"I'm worried about the newspaper industry."

Depression

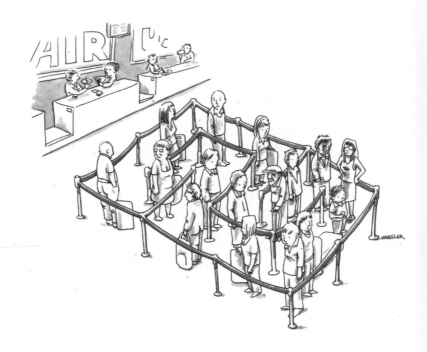

Depression

"*With a small surgery we can reverse the effects of your bloated bank account.*"

Depression

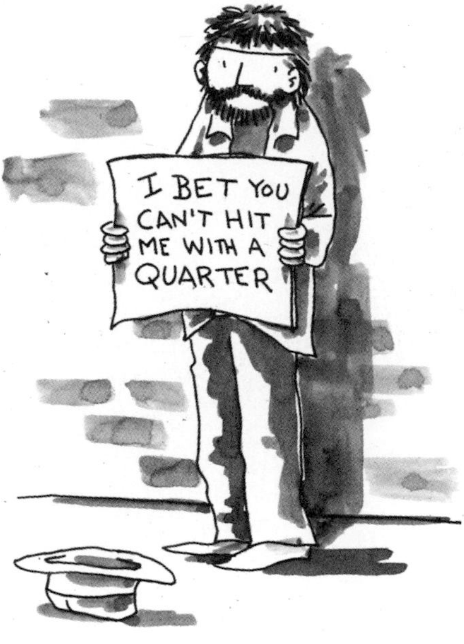
I BET YOU
CAN'T HIT
ME WITH A
QUARTER

"I never should have trusted that rat."

89

Depression

"What are you in for?"

Depression

"He uses performance-suppressing drugs."

Depression

"I take my job too seriously."

Depression

"For two months coffee will be bad for you. Then
it will be good for you for six months. Then it will be bad
for you for three weeks. Then good for you in Europe but
bad for you in the United States. Then it will be good."

Depression

"I don't care if it's our best china. It's still cat food."

Depression

"Please don't worry. It's normal for your son to talk."

Depression

OR·NOT·GASM

Depression

Depression

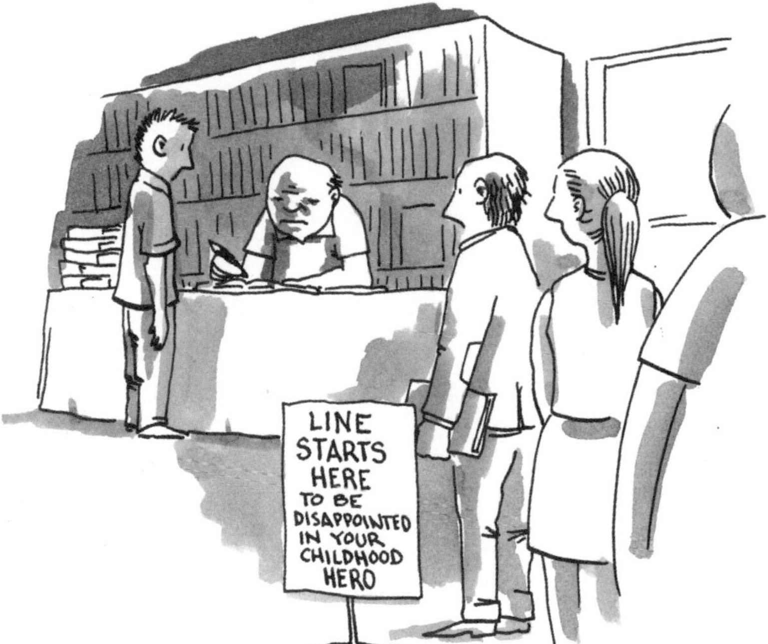
LINE
STARTS
HERE
TO BE
DISAPPOINTED
IN YOUR
CHILDHOOD
HERO

"NSFW."

Depression

ACCEPTANCE

"I'm just here for the cable."

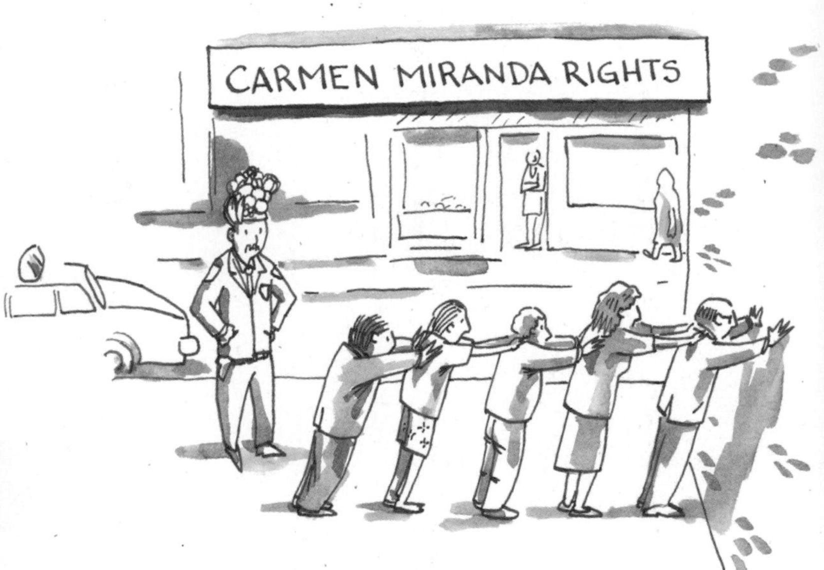
CARMEN MIRANDA RIGHTS

*"Getting paid with exposure
isn't nearly as bad as I thought."*

Acceptance

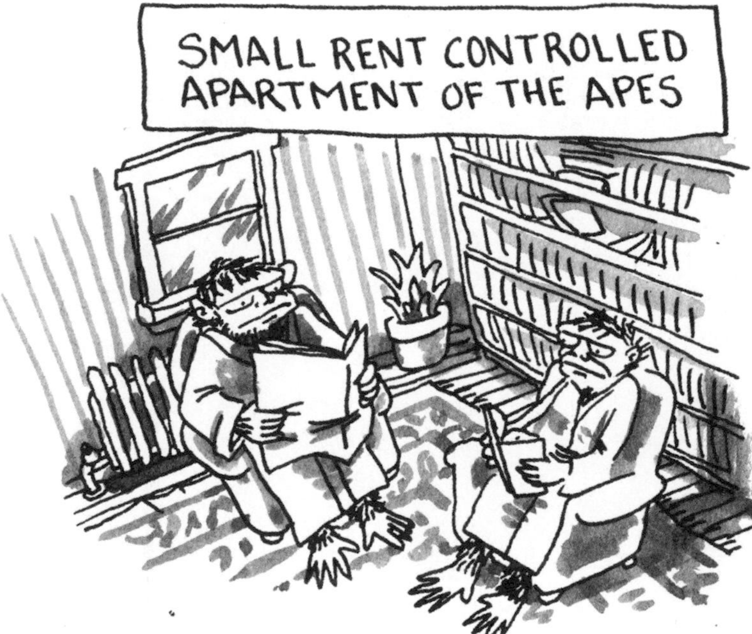
SMALL RENT CONTROLLED
APARTMENT OF THE APES

"*When I grow up I want
to be a content provider.*"

Acceptance

"Nice. 3-D printing."

Acceptance

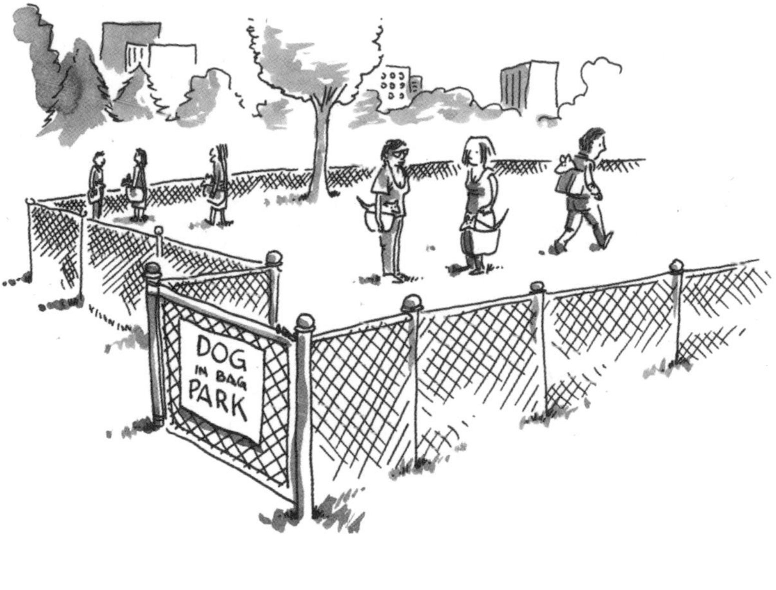
DOG
IN BAG
PARK

"The sound effects are here."

Acceptance

"I can't help wondering what the mice are doing."

Acceptance

"Thanks for contributing humorous material for my upcoming one-woman show."

Acceptance

"I love when my car has that new pizza smell."

Acceptance

"I'm thinking about having some Photoshop done."

Acceptance

"You're cured."

Acceptance

"Bouncy castle."

Acceptance

"*Remember, it's the journey,
not the destination.*"

Acceptance

Running wild with an unused degree in architecture and an Eisner Award, Shannon Wheeler lives in Portland, Oregon, where he has cartooned for magazines such as *The New Yorker* and *The Onion*. He's best known for his creation *Too Much Coffee Man*. The cartoons in this book are available for use for a nominal fee; write to shannoncartoons@gmail.com. You can also contact him at cartoons@tmcm.com, or visit his website: www.tmcm.com.

Other books by Shannon Wheeler

I Thought You Would Be Funnier
I Told You So
Too Much Coffee Man
How To Be Happy
Screw Heaven, When I Die I'm Going to Mars
Postage Stamp Funnies

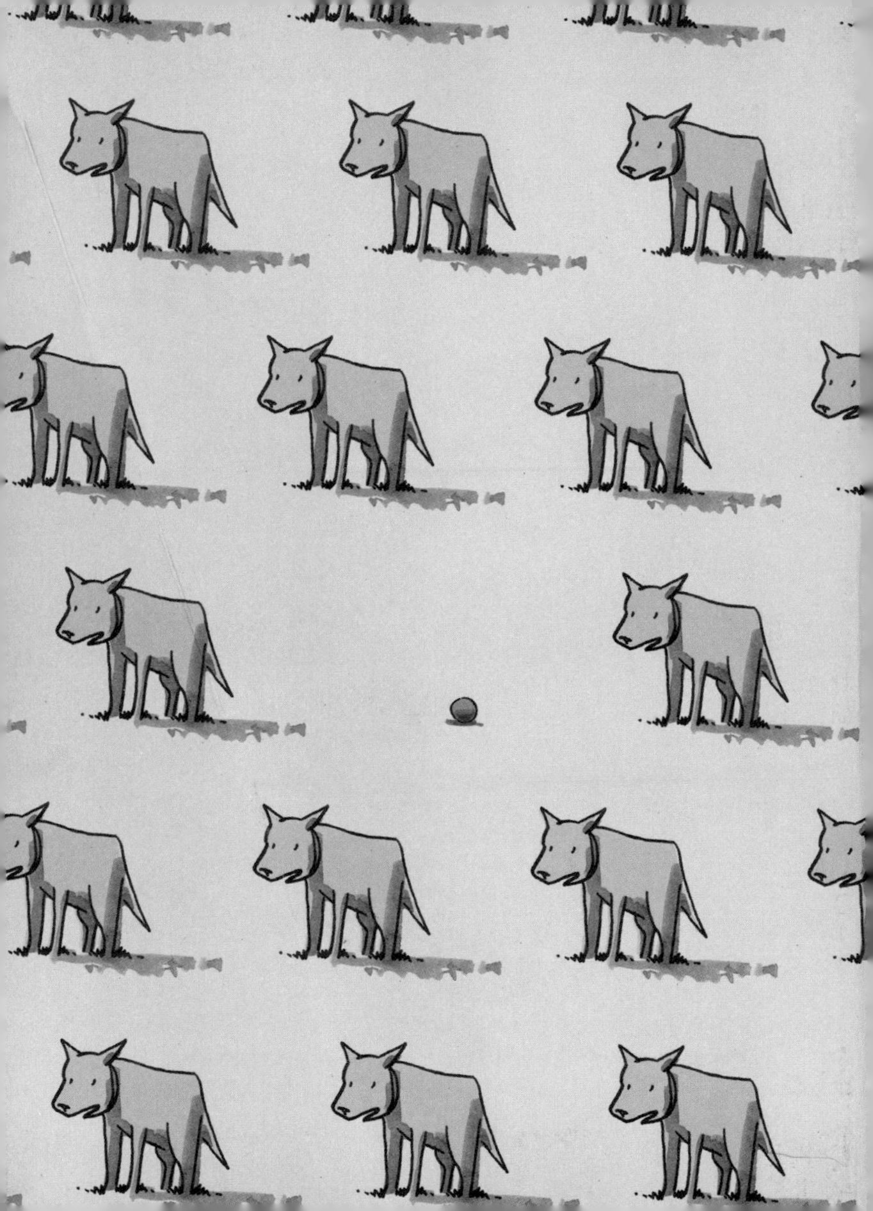